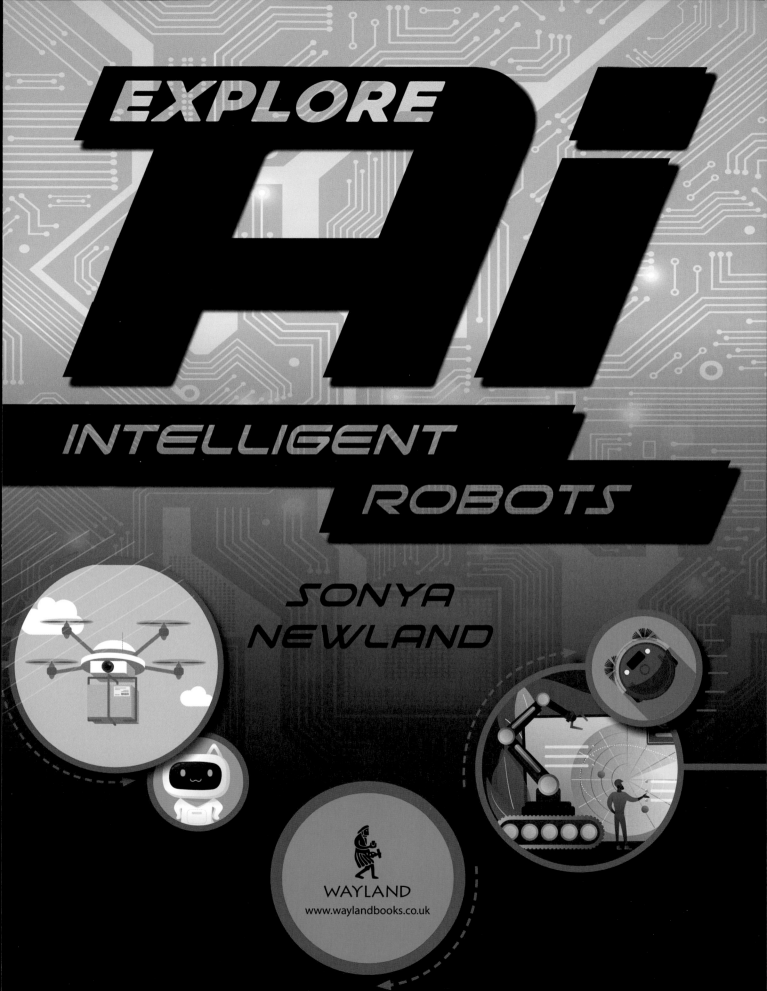

EXPLORE AI

INTELLIGENT ROBOTS

SONYA NEWLAND

WAYLAND
www.waylandbooks.co.uk

First published in Great Britain in 2021 by Wayland

Copyright © Hodder & Stoughton Limited, 2021

Produced for Wayland by
White-Thomson Publishing Ltd
www.wtpub.co.uk

Editor: Sonya Newland
Designer: Dan Prescott, Couper Street Type Co.

HB ISBN: 978 1 5263 1510 6
PB ISBN: 978 1 5263 1515 1
10 9 8 7 6 5 4 3 2

Wayland
An imprint of Hachette Children's Group
Part of Hodder & Stoughton
Carmelite House
50 Victoria Embankment
London EC4Y 0DZ

An Hachette UK Company
www.hachette.co.uk
www.hachettechildrens.co.uk

Printed in Dubai

You can find words in **bold**
in the glossary on page 30.

The publisher would like to thank the following for permission to reproduce their pictures:
Alamy: Haruyoshi Yamaguchi/AFLO/Alamy Live News 8t, Everett Collection Inc 8b, World History Archive 14b, dpa picture alliance 15, Silas Stein/dpa 17t, Cavan 20b, Guy Bell 29t; Getty Images: Bettmann 7t, John Pratt 7b, Ralph Crane 11t, Leon Neal 28; NASA: JSC 14t; Shutterstock: ProStockStudio 4, Bluehousestudio 5t, Artist_R 5b, Vlad Kochelaevskiy 6t, studioworkstock 6bl, Meilun 6br, Mykola Holyutyak 9, Tatiana Shepeleva 10t, Robert Voight 10b, Olena Yakobchuk 11b, Ico Maker 12–13, 17b, Roi and Roi 12b, Morphart creation 13b, elenabsl 16, 18–19, viper-zero 17m, NadzeyaShanchuk 20t, VikiVector 21t, Robert Kneschke 21b, MikeDotta 22t, kvector 22b, Miriam Doerr Martin Frommherz 23t, tanyabosyk 23b, airdone 24t, Anastasiia Kozubenko 24b, Phonlamai Photo 25t, VectorSun 25b, Nadia Snopek 26t, Anton Gvozdikov 26b, Zenzen 27, Gaming Logo 29b.

All design elements from Shutterstock.

CONTENTS

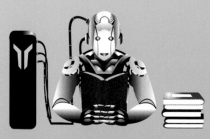

WHAT IS AI?

Artificial Intelligence (AI) is the science, technology and engineering of intelligent machines. AI is all around you – a part of your everyday life. A lot of the time you might not even realise that the devices you interact with are 'intelligent'!

AMAZING AI ABILITIES

The goal of AI is to create machines that use human-like intelligence to perform many different tasks. These might be practical jobs, such as mowing the lawn. But they may also be incredibly tricky tasks where the machine has to think and learn.

HUMANS – THE ULTIMATE MACHINES

Your brain is an amazing machine, carrying out complex processes every second of every day. It's how you think, feel, react, reason, analyse, learn and explain. Understanding human abilities like these is key to AI – recreating these processes in machines is what makes artificial intelligence so 'real'.

WHAT ARE AI ROBOTS?

Robots are machines that do work. They can take the form of anything that saves humans time and effort doing the task themselves. An *intelligent* robot is one that understands, learns and adapts its behaviour on its own, without having to be reprogrammed by a human.

ROBOT TAKEOVER?

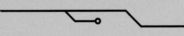

As scientists and engineers work to make robots smarter, some people have started to wonder what the dangers of creating intelligent robots might be. Just because we *can* create human-like robots, does that mean we *should*? AI engineers consider **ethical** questions carefully in their work. For example, what if robots evolve to become cleverer than humans? What rights should robots have if they can think and feel just like us?

ROBOTICS AND AI

The word 'robot' was coined in 1920 by the Czech writer Karel Čapek. He used it in his play *Rossum's Universal Robots*. Čapek's robots were the first to try to take over the world!

WHAT'S THE DIFFERENCE?

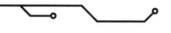

We tend to think of robots as being a bit like humans, and they are often pictured in **humanoid** form. Because of this, it's easy to assume that all robots have artificial intelligence. But **robotics** isn't always the same thing as AI.

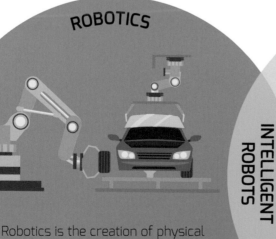

ROBOTICS

Robotics is the creation of physical robots – programmable machines that do work, such as the robots that assemble cars on a factory **production line**.

INTELLIGENT ROBOTS

AI

AI robots are robots that are controlled by AI technology. They think, learn and **adapt** on their own.

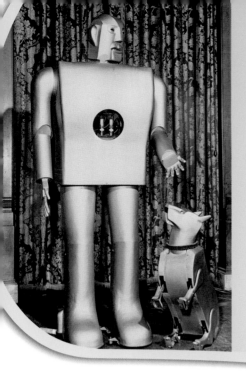

A ROBOT'S BEST FRIEND

The first-ever **automated** robot was called Elektro. It was unveiled at the 1939 World's Fair, a special exhibition in New York, USA, that showed great achievements from around the globe. Elektro was a 2.1-m tall humanoid robot. It responded to voice commands and could walk, move its head and arms, and speak about 700 words!

Elektro starred at the World's Fair again the following year, along with Sparko, a robot dog that could bark, sit and beg.

AI DEVELOPS

As the idea of AI began to spread, engineers realised that robots were the perfect form for intelligent machines. Experts began looking for ways to build autonomous robots – ones that would not simply respond to instructions, but which would learn from their own mistakes.

BRIGHT MINDS

William Grey Walter (1910–77) thought that robots might help doctors to understand how the human brain works. He built several animal robots that he called 'tortoises' (a play on the words 'taught us', from *Alice in Wonderland*). They were designed to see how a small number of 'brain cells' could make machines behave in complex ways. The **neuroscience** element of Walter's ideas is not widely respected these days, but he had a big influence on robotics.

Elmer and Elsie were two of Walter's 'tortoise' robots. They were built in 1948–49 and were the first robots programmed to think in a way similar to humans. Using their three wheels, they moved towards or away from light. They could even find their own way to a charging station when their batteries were low!

AI IN ACTION

I, ROBOT

At first, the idea of AI was based on building computers that could use processes like the ones that take place in the human brain. But experts soon realised that computers had physical limitations. What if they could create *robots* that would be able to use those processes instead?

ASIMOV'S VISION

In 1950, American writer Isaac Asimov (1920–92) published a collection of stories called *I, Robot*. This famous science-fiction book brought the idea of intelligent robots to the wider public. People began to get excited about what robots might be able to do to help humans.

Early ideas about creating humanoid robots are now a reality. 'Cybernetic humans' have been built – and they're very lifelike!

Isaac Asimov was a science professor as well as a science-fiction writer.

Asimov also came up with the idea of a computer that could store every single piece of human knowledge. It would be able to answer any question a person asked! Such a computer hasn't been invented yet, of course.

RULES FOR ROBOTS

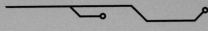

Asimov invented the Three Laws of Robotics, which were designed to prevent robots turning against their human inventors. Although they were written as a piece of fiction, these laws still influence the ethics of AI robotics today.

THE THREE LAWS OF ROBOTICS

1   A robot may not injure a human being or, through inaction, allow a human being to come to harm.

2   A robot must obey the orders given it by human beings except where such orders would conflict with the First Law.

3   A robot must protect its own existence as long as such protection does not conflict with the First or Second Laws.

WHAT IF...? What if robots really did have the same level of intelligence as humans? Is a robot takeover something we should worry about? Asimov always said that if humans were ever clever enough to create intelligent robots, they would be clever enough to make sure the robots wouldn't (or couldn't) turn against them. Do you think he was right?

DOES THIS MAKE SENSE?

One of the first automated tasks robots were able to perform was finding their way around obstacles. After all, if a machine couldn't move without bumping into things, it wasn't going to be much help to humans!

SAFETY STOP OR CRASH LAND?

Put an intelligent and a non-intelligent robot on a table and set them moving. What happens when they reach the edge? The ordinary robot – with no 'mind' of its own – will topple off the table. The intelligent robot is aware of its surroundings, so it will stop at the edge.

MAKING SENSE OF THINGS

To find their way around, early automated robots like Walter's 'tortoises' (see page 7) followed a light. Soon, engineers also developed a 'bump' **sensor**. The idea of these 'sensory' **inputs** was that they were similar to the human senses of sight and touch. They helped the robot react to particular things in its environment.

Amazingly, the way scientists saw the senses of sight and touch working together in robots helped them develop a better understanding of the human **nervous system**.

10

'Shakey' was built in 1969 and was the first robot that could decide its own actions by mapping its surroundings. Shakey was all very well in theory, but in practice it was not a great success. The robot moved very slowly and was easily confused by any unusual objects it came across!

SEE, HEAR, TOUCH, TASTE, SMELL

Today, AI engineers have found ways to give robots some form of human senses. Many intelligent robots can see and hear, talk and move. The real challenge is not only to give intelligent robots human senses, but to get the different senses working together in the way that ours do. Only then can the robot fully understand and respond to its environment.

Although robots have some human-like senses, realistic senses of smell and taste have been more difficult to recreate in machines. Do you think these senses are important in robots?

You've probably interacted with a hearing robot. Do you ever ask Siri a question or give Alexa an order? These virtual personal assistants hear and respond to your voice.

FIVE SENSES

HUMANS...

Humans have five basic senses: sight, hearing, smell, touch and taste. Our sensory organs – our eyes, ears, nose, skin and tongue – interact with things and send messages to our brain. This is how we perceive and understand the world around us.

SIGHT: Light is reflected off an object and into our eyes. There, it is bent and focused on the **retina**, which is full of **nerve cells**. The cells turn the light into vision and motion, and the information is sent to the brain through the **optic nerve**.

HEARING: Sound waves hit the ear drum, causing it to vibrate. The vibrations travel to a hearing receptor, which turns them into electrical signals. The signals travel to the brain via sensory nerves.

SMELL: We smell by inhaling air that contains odour **molecules**. Receptors then send messages to the parts of the brain that interpret scent.

TOUCH: Receptors in our skin send information about the object we are touching to our brain. We feel temperature, pressure, pain, movement and many other sensations in this way.

TASTE: We can identify five different tastes: sweet, salty, sour, bitter and umami (savoury). These are all sensed via the taste buds on the tongue.

Humans can distinguish between more than a trillion different scents thanks to their 400 smelling receptors.

...VS. MACHINES

At the moment, even intelligent robots don't sense their environment in a 'real' way. But AI engineers have come up with some ingenious alternatives to human sense processes which allow robots to react to their environment.

SIGHT: Robot vision comes from video cameras. These collect images that are fed to a computer processor (the robot's 'brain').

HEARING: Microphones allow intelligent robots to 'hear', but AI engineers are also working on ways for robots to understand sounds in the way we do. HEARBO is a robot that can identify and process different types of sound, including voices.

SMELL: Sensors could 'receive' scents like our noses can. Researchers in Mexico have developed an 'e-nose', which can identify certain smells. It uses **algorithms** to work out where the smell is and move towards that place.

TOUCH: AI engineers are working on a 'smart skin' for robots. This would contain thousands of sensors that could detect things like force and temperature.

TASTE: This may seem like the least useful sense for a robot, but robots that can taste would have many uses. They could taste food for people with severe allergies. They could also ensure that food labels accurately state what is in a product.

At the moment, robots can recognise only four or five specific odours that they have been 'taught' to identify.

13

ROBONAUTS

Robonauts are a special kind of intelligent robot. These 'astronaut robots' are designed to help humans travel to, explore and understand worlds beyond our own. Their human-like senses of touch and sight help them do this.

NASA'S ROBONAUTS

The first robonauts looked like the top half of a human, with a head, body and arms. More recent versions sometimes have two 'climbing manipulators' – or legs. They are designed to do the same type of tasks that astronauts do when they are out in space.

HOW DOES A ROBONAUT WORK?

The arms are able to lift up to 10 kg, and they never get tired!

The hands and fingers move in the same way as a human's, so it can do things like holding and using tools.

Cameras in the robonaut's head allow it to 'see' everything around it.

The robonaut's power unit is stored in its backpack.

WHAT IF...? What if one day space exploration can be done entirely by intelligent robots? Does that defeat the point of it? Is the idea simply to learn about our universe, or is it important for humans to experience life in space for themselves? Would the Moon landing in 1969 have been so amazing if it had been humanoid robots that made that 'one small step'?

MEET THE CIMONS

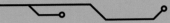

CIMON (**C**rew **I**nteractive **M**obile Compani**on**) was the first space bot with an AI brain! This head-shaped robot went to the International Space Station (ISS) in 2018, where it spent 14 months working with astronauts. It showed how humans and robots can work together in space. The updated CIMON 2 was launched to the ISS in 2019.

The German chancellor Angela Merkel meets the CIMON robot before it leaves for its first mission to the ISS.

The AI used in the CIMON robots is IBM's Watson **software**. Watson was one of the first intelligent computers – able to beat humans at the American quiz show *Jeopardy!*

CAN I HELP YOU?

Some people are already worried about robots becoming so intelligent that they will take over all the jobs that humans do. But, right now, robots are proving very useful in doing tasks that are dangerous for people.

SAFETY FIRST

Ordinary industrial robots were designed to do jobs such as **welding** or lifting and moving heavy materials – tasks that were difficult or dangerous for humans in factories. But industrial robots could be dangerous for people to work near. Engineers began to think of ways to create industrial robots that could operate safely alongside human workers. And so, the cobot – the collaborative robot – was born!

BRIGHT MINDS

American mechanical engineers J. Edward Colgate and Michael Peskin were the brains behind the first cobot, invented in 1996. They wanted to design a computer-controlled robot that could interact directly with people in the workplace. To do so, they had to carefully consider not only what jobs the cobot might need to do, but also factors such as the materials used to build them.

16

CLEVER COBOTS

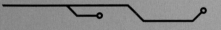

Cobots use their AI programming to detect changes in their working environment and change their behaviour accordingly. They can also adapt the job they are doing. For example, if they are assembling a product, they can 'see' what they are working on and adapt to choose the correct pieces. Cobots can identify patterns in a particular process, so they can predict when things might go wrong.

Cobots are made of lightweight materials and have smooth surfaces and round shapes rather than sharp corners. These features make them safe co-workers.

MILITARY ASSISTANCE

Another area where AI robots are helping humans is in the military. Soldiers face very difficult and dangerous situations, so intelligent robots can be really useful. PackBots are used in war zones. They can help with bomb disposal and in finding survivors trapped in rubble after natural disasters, such as earthquakes. Thanks to AI technology, PackBots can create their own maps of the landscape and choose the best route to follow.

BigDog was a military robot invented to carry supplies for soldiers working in rough terrains. Because it had four legs like a real dog, it could cross difficult landscapes more easily than a wheeled vehicle. It could move at different speeds and in different ways. In the end, BigDog was too loud to be useful, but the next generation, SpotMini, has been more successful!

AI
IN ACTION

COOPERATION

HUMANS...

Humans are quite contradictory! On the one hand, we can be selfish and competitive. But on the other hand, we have an in-built instinct to cooperate and **collaborate** – to help one another. Humans have skills that are particularly suited to cooperation.

ADAPTABILITY: We can adjust to changes in our environment or working conditions.

SOCIAL SKILLS: We can interact in a friendly, social way with other people, to make cooperating easier and more enjoyable.

LEADERSHIP: We can take charge, organising other people to get a job done efficiently.

CREATIVITY: We can 'think outside the box', using our imagination to come up with new ideas.

TEAMWORK: We can discuss and debate ideas, deciding as a team the best approach to a task.

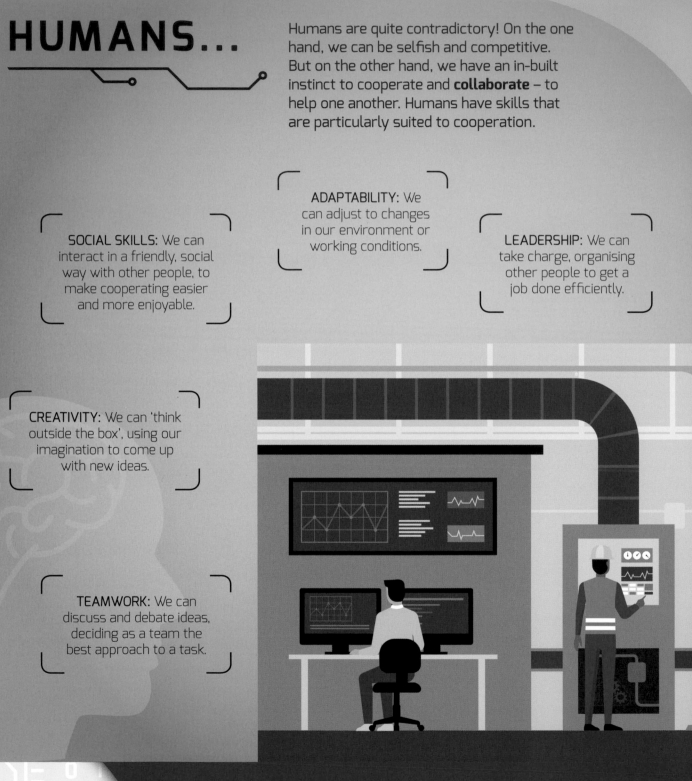

Robots do not have all the same collaborative skills as humans. But they can be programmed with features that are similar to human skills, or which work well alongside ours.

...VS. MACHINES

ADAPTABILITY: AI machines can respond to changes in conditions, adapting their behaviour accordingly.

LEADERSHIP: AI robots are able to control other robots and machines.

ANALYTICAL SKILLS: Robots can analyse information much more quickly and accurately than humans.

TIRELESSNESS: However fast or long they work, machines never get tired!

SPEED: Robots can work quickly and efficiently.

ROBOT PETS

Humans have always had a close relationship with animals. We use them for many different purposes, including as companions. Some AI engineers are using what we know about animal behaviour to develop new technology. This mimics animals' best and most useful characteristics.

ANIMAL INTELLIGENCE

AI experts often look at how animals behave to give them ideas for developing different types of intelligence. For example, creatures like ants show an amazing intelligence in the way they work together to build a nest and gather food.

Apes are like humans in many ways, but they don't have the same type of intelligence as we do. However, this makes them easier to mimic. Some scientists think that this could be a good stepping stone for developing human-like artificial intelligence

In his futuristic novel *Do Androids Dream of Electric Sheep?* Philip K. Dick imagined a world where most people had been forced to move to other planets. The people left on Earth keep android animals as pets, which are highly prized!

CATS AND DOGS

There are many different robot versions of our favourite companions – cats and dogs. Some of these use artificial intelligence, including special sensors, cameras and **actuators** (parts of a machine that control movement). For example, AIBO (**A**rtifical **I**ntelligence Ro**bo**t) is a range of robotic dogs that can learn tricks and respond to their owner's personality.

AI IN ACTION

DragonBot is a **social robot** that has been developed to help children learn. Its inventors describe it as a 'personalised learning companion'. It works on a mobile phone and uses the camera and microphone to 'see' and 'speak'. Because it is connected to the internet, information can be shared between robots.

WHAT IF...? What if all children had access to a 'learning companion' like DragonBot? Is this a good thing that might improve learning ability and intelligence? What drawbacks might there be? Is it good to have robotic companions, or is it more important for young children to interact with human friends?

HOW DO YOU FEEL?

Emotions are unique to us as human beings. Although some animals seem to show feelings, as far as we are aware, only humans are capable of a wide range of emotions. So, how are AI engineers creating robots with *emotional* intelligence?

DO EMOTIONS GET IN THE WAY?

How we feel about things and how we react to situations are all part of our personality. But some people think that emotions are preventing humans evolving further. For example, does fear keep us safe from things that might cause us harm? Or does it hold us back, stopping us trying things that wouldn't hurt us at all if only we gave them a go?

If AI engineers are hoping to create a robotic 'superhuman', would it be better if it *didn't* have emotions?

WHAT IF...? What if scientists could create a robot that had the intelligence of a human but none of our emotions? What consequences might there be? Are there advantages to having no emotions? What dangers or drawbacks might there be?

ARTIFICIAL EMPATHY

Empathy is the ability to identify with someone else's feelings. It allows us to see the world through their eyes, to understand and help them. People such as care workers often have a lot of empathy, but jobs like this can be emotionally very difficult for the workers. Now, AI researchers have developed software that creates 'artificial empathy'. If robots can be truly empathetic, they can help to take care of vulnerable people who need patience and understanding.

Some empathy robots may be specially designed to help take care of elderly people.

Romeo is a robot designed to help older people who are no longer able to do some of the things that they used to do. Romeo can recognise faces and perform many basic but useful tasks, such as opening doors, compiling shopping lists and remembering appointments. There are plans for Romeo to be a true companion, too – able to play games and have conversations.

AI
IN ACTION

CAN ROBOTS FALL IN LOVE?

Developmental robotics is the field of AI that focuses on robots that learn and develop in the way humans do. One day, this might lead to robots that can learn emotional behaviour from humans. A lot of our interactions and relationships already happen online instead of face to face. So, is it so strange to think that sometime in the future half your friends could be robots? Would you even know?!

EMOTIONS

HUMANS...

Human emotions are very complicated! They are a result of many factors, from **hormones** in our bodies to emotions triggered by memories of things that have happened in the past. We experience emotions when chemical levels change in the body. This activates different parts of the brain, which causes different responses.

LOVE/TRUST: Oxytocin is released when we are physically close to another person. It helps us form strong social bonds.

HAPPINESS: Serotonin is released when we exercise or go out in the sunshine. This chemical controls our moods, keeping us happy. It also helps us sleep well.

MOTIVATION: Dopamine is a natural chemical that is very **addictive**! It's what makes you want to keep doing things that feel good or that have positive benefits.

FEAR/EXCITEMENT: The hormone adrenaline increases the flow of blood to the muscles, raises the heart rate and puts us on high alert.

Humans experience more than 25 distinct emotions, triggered by chemicals in the body.

...VS. MACHINES

FACIAL EXPRESSIONS: Robots can be programmed to identify certain facial expressions and link them with an emotion. For example, an intelligent robot might recognise that a downturned mouth and tears mean that someone is sad.

Machines have no body, no hormones and no real memory in a human sense. Some robots can understand human emotions, but at the moment no robots exist that can actually *feel* those emotions themselves. However, AI engineers have created robots that mimic human emotions very convincingly!

PHYSICAL CUES: Just as we respond to physical cues in our body, so robots could learn to do so. For example, a low battery level could result in feelings of lethargy or a high temperature could cause 'angry' behaviour.

EXTERNAL DATA: Intelligent robots could interpret and analyse data and give an appropriate emotional response. For example, if a robot supported a particular football team, its reaction to a match win would be one of celebration!

Robots cannot 'feel' emotions because they have no hormones in their bodies.

THE ETHICS OF ROBOTICS

All AI comes with a lot of big questions, but the rise of intelligent robots is one area that has really got people thinking about the rights and wrongs of AI. Roboethics is the field of study that explores how humans should behave as they design, build and use artificially intelligent beings.

RIGHTS FOR ROBOTS

In 2017, the European Parliament agreed that there should be a set of laws that outlined robot rights. These laws would decide how artificial intelligence and robots should be developed and used. Early drafts of the laws included some basic rights and rules for robots. One of these is a state of 'electronic personhood' for the most advanced intelligent robots, making them legally recognised beings.

HUMAN RIGHTS

ROBOT RIGHTS

Sophia became the world's first robot 'person' in 2017, when she became a citizen of Saudi Arabia. Sophia looks and acts very much like a human. She has more than 60 facial expressions, and she is able to learn human gestures that make her very lifelike.

AI IN ACTION

MACHINE ETHICS

Ethical issues aren't just about how humans should treat robots. Ethics also need to consider rules that govern the way robots themselves should behave. This raises another question – should we be teaching robots right from wrong? Or should AI engineers be trying to design intelligent robots that have *their own* set of ethics? If robots don't decide their own laws like we do, can we say they're truly intelligent?

RIGHT OR WRONG?

Where do we draw the line in intelligent robots? AI can be used in many different areas, including in medicine, healthcare and the military. There is no doubt that intelligent robots can improve and even save lives. But they may also be used to harm others. Is that acceptable?

WHAT IF...? What if, one day soon, robots are able to experience a wide range of human emotions? Does that change how we should treat them? Is that the point at which they stop being machines and start being true cousins to the human race? If so, should they have the same rights and legal protections as we do? How might that threaten our own rights?

THE FUTURE OF ROBOTICS

Robotics began as a mission to help people with dull, difficult or dangerous jobs, but today AI is taking robotics beyond work. Researchers are now developing robots with emotional and creative abilities.

CREATIVE THINKING

One day the world's great poets, playwrights, artists and composers might be robots! In 2019, the world's first robotic artist, Ai-Da, held an exhibition at Oxford University in England. To create her art, Ai-Da draws a basic picture. Humans then use an algorithm that 'reads' the image and turns it into a more complex piece of art. This is then printed out on a canvas.

Ai-Da the robot artist at work.

WHAT IF...? What if robots really do become the artists of the future? Is art created by robots really art? Or does art have to come from a human mind? How should we define 'creativity'? Would you want to go to an exhibition of art created by machines?

LIFELIKE ROBOTS

Engineers are working on creating robots that are increasingly lifelike to look at. They give them natural-looking hair and skin – sometimes the skin can even trigger a reaction to a human touch in the robot. Designers hope that this will break down barriers between humans and machines.

Some intelligent robots have eyes that blink and pupils that get bigger and smaller in the dark and light the way that ours do.

ROBOT EDUCATION

One of the key things for a successful future in robotics is for robots to become more self-sufficient. They need to learn for themselves. Some robots can already do this. For example, a robot called Brett taught itself about shapes by practising using a child's shape-sorting toy! This is the way that humans learn things.

BRIGHT MINDS

Rodney Brooks (b. 1954) is an Australian roboticist. He wrote a paper called 'Elephants Don't Play Chess', which said it was more important for artificially intelligent robots to be able to move, think and act within an environment – to do 'common-sense' things – than it was for them to be able to compute detailed information. Brooks later founded Rethink Robotics, which aims to create affordable robots.

GLOSSARY

actuator – the part of a machine that controls its movement

adapt – to change to meet new conditions

addictive – describes things that you want to keep doing because they make you feel good

algorithm – a set of steps that tell a computer what to do in order to solve a problem or perform a task

automated – describes things that are operated by automatic processes

collaborate – to work with others to achieve a common goal

empathy – the ability to understand and share someone else's feelings

ethical – relating to whether things are right or wrong

hormone – a substance in the body that triggers physical and emotional reactions

humanoid – describes thing that have the same basic form and shape as a human

input – the information put into a computer

molecule – a group of atoms joined together to create the smallest unit of a chemical

nerve cell – a cell that carries messages around the body and to the brain in the form of electrical impulses

nervous system – the network of cells and fibres that carry electrical impulses around the body, to and from the brain

neuroscience – the study of how the brain and nervous system are connected and work in the human body

optic nerve – the nerve that carries electrical signals from the retina in the eye to the brain

production line – a system in a factory where the product being made passes through a fixed sequence of steps

retina – the part of the eye that contains light-sensitive cells

robotics – the branch of technology that deals with designing and building robots

sensor – a device that detects and responds to physical things

social robot – a robot that is designed to interact with humans and other robots

software – the programs that give computers the instructions they need to work

welding – joining pieces of metal by heating the surfaces with a flame

FIND OUT MORE

BOOKS

AI (The Tech-Head Guide) by William Potter (Wayland, 2020)

Robots (Adventures in STEAM) by Izzi Howell (Wayland, 2019)

Robots (The Tech-Head Guide) by William Potter (Wayland, 2020)

Working with Computers and Robotics (Kid Engineer) by Sonya Newland (Wayland, 2020)

WEBSITES

www.bbc.co.uk/newsround/49274918

Discover more about what AI is and what it does.

https://science.howstuffworks.com/robot6.htm

Find out about the relationships between robots and AI.

INDEX

EXPLORE AI